The Sea-Wolf
Jack London

Abridged and adapted by Tony Napoli

Illustrated by Steve Moore

A PACEMAKER CLASSIC

GLOBE FEARON
EDUCATIONAL PUBLISHER
PARAMUS, NEW JERSEY

Paramount Publishing

Supervising Editor: Stephen Feinstein
Project Editor: Karen Bernhaut
Editorial Assistant: Stacie Dozier
Art Director: Nancy Sharkey
Assistant Art Director: Armando Baéz
Production Manager: Penny Gibson
Production Editor: Nicole Cypher
Desktop Specialist: Eric Dawson
Manufacturing Supervisor: Della Smith
Marketing Manager: Marge Curson
Cover Illustration: Steve Moore

Copyright © 1995 by Globe Fearon Educational Publisher, a division of Paramount Publishing, 240 Frisch Court, Paramus, New Jersey 07652. All rights reserved. No part of this book may be reproduced or transmitted in any form or by any means, electrical or mechanical, including photocopying, recording, o by any information storage and retrieval system, without permission in writing from the publisher.

Printed in the United States of America
1 2 3 4 5 6 7 8 9 10 99 98 97 96 95 94

ISBN 0–835–90969–7

GLOBE FEARON
EDUCATIONAL PUBLISHER
PARAMUS, NEW JERSEY

Paramount Publishing

Contents

1	Stranded at Sea	1
2	Life Aboard the *Ghost*	11
3	A Nightmare of Brutality	21
4	A Murderous Plot	32
5	Rescued from a Storm	40
6	Death in the Water	48
7	A Silent Understanding	56
8	Escape!	62
9	Endeavor Island	70
10	An Unwelcome Visitor	75
11	Repairing the *Ghost*	81
12	A Return to the Open Sea	88

Cast of Characters

Humphrey Van Weyden	The narrator; a rescued passenger from a sunken ferry boat who becomes an unwilling crew member on the *Ghost*
Wolf Larsen	The cruel and brutal captain of the *Ghost*
Thomas Mugridge	The bitter and ignorant cook aboard the *Ghost*
Johansen	The first mate aboard the *Ghost* who always obeys Captain Larsen's orders
Louis	A crew member of the *Ghost* who befriends Van Weyden
Johnson and Leach	Two rebellious sailors who become bitter enemies of Wolf Larsen
Death Larsen	Wolf Larsen's brother and captain of the steamship *Macedonia*, another sealing vessel
Maud Brewster	A well-bred author who was rescued by the *Ghost* after a typhoon

1   Stranded at Sea

I hardly know where to begin. Sometimes I place the cause of it all to Charley Furuseth. I was in the habit of visiting him on weekends at his cottage in Mill Valley across the bay from San Francisco. In the course of returning from one of these visits, I found myself one January morning afloat in San Francisco Bay.

There was a heavy fog that morning. But I had no special fear of being out in the water. I was traveling in a safe craft, the *Martinez*. It was one of those new ferry steamers. I took up my position on the forward upper deck, right below the pilothouse. A fresh breeze was blowing, and the mystery of the fog took hold of my thoughts.

A red-faced man slammed the cabin door behind him and stomped out on deck. He interrupted my thoughts. "It's nasty weather like this that turns heads gray before their time," he said. He nodded toward the pilothouse.

From out of the fog came the mournful tolling of a bell. I could see the pilot turning the wheel with great speed. Our own whistle was blowing, and from time to time the sound of other whistles came to us out of the fog.

"Hello, somebody's comin' our way," the newcomer said. "He's comin' fast, too. Guess he don't hear us yet. Wind is blowing in the wrong direction."

"A ferryboat?" I asked.

He nodded. Then he added, "They're getting nervous up there."

I looked up. The captain had stuck his head and shoulders out of the pilothouse. He was staring deeply into the fog as if by sheer force of will he could see through it.

Then everything happened with great speed. The fog broke away, and the bow of a steamboat emerged. A white-bearded man leaned out of its pilothouse. He seemed to accept his fate. He looked us over with a calm eye. And he took no notice when our pilot, white with rage, shouted, "Now you've done it."

The vessels came together before I could grab hold of something. We must have been struck squarely amidships, for I saw nothing. The strange steamboat had passed my line of vision. The *Martinez* heeled over sharply, and there was a crashing of timber. I was thrown flat on the wet deck. I heard the screams of the women.

I tried to reach the life preservers but was thrown back by a wild rush of men and women. I finally grabbed a life preserver and ran off to the lower deck. The *Martinez* was sinking. One lifeboat was lowered with the plugs out. When the women and children got in, the boat quickly capsized. Other passengers were leaping overboard. Some, already in the water, were screaming to be taken aboard again. Seized by panic, I went over the side in a rush of bodies.

The water was cold—so cold that it was painful. It filled my lungs until the life preserver popped me to the surface. The taste of salt water was strong in my mouth. But it was the cold that was the worst. I felt I could survive only a few minutes. I heard a final chorus of screams and knew that the *Martinez* had gone down.

Later—I don't know how much later—my head cleared a little. I was alone. I could hear no calls or cries, only the sounds of the waves. I felt as if I was being carried out to sea.

I went black for awhile. Then I became aware of a vessel above me with three triangular sails. I tried to reach it as it passed me by, but I could not. I tried to call out for help but could not make a sound.

A moment later, one of the two men at the wheel caught sight of me. He whirled the wheel around and began shouting orders. I felt myself blacking out again. A little later I heard the stroke of oars. Then the darkness rose over me.

I seemed to be having a dream. I was being jerked back and forth with great speed. I was being dragged over rough sands, hot in the sun. It all gave me a feeling of tremendous pain.

I gasped, caught my breath, and opened my eyes. Two men were kneeling beside me, working over me. The jerking motion was the lift and forward plunge of a ship. The hot sands were a man's hard hands scraping my naked chest. I squirmed under the pain and half lifted my head.

"That will do, Yonson," one of the men said. "You've just about rubbed the man's skin off."

The man who had spoken was British—a cockney. From the way he was dressed, I could tell he was the ship's cook. And I seemed to be lying in the ship's dirty galley.

"And how are you feelin' now, sir," he asked.

Without answering, I got weakly into a sitting position. Then Yonson helped me to my feet. I glanced down to my raw, bleeding chest.

"Thank you, Mr. Yonson," I said.

"My name is Johnson, not Yonson," he said. He spoke in very good, though slow, English. It had just a shade of a Scandinavian accent to it.

"Thank you, Mr. Johnson," I said. I turned to the cook. "Do you have any clothes I may put on?"

"Yes sir," he said. "If you don't object to wearing my things. I'll run and take a look."

"And where am I?" I asked Johnson. "What vessel is this and where is it bound?"

"Off the Farallons, heading about southwest," he answered. "The schooner *Ghost*, bound for seal-hunting to Japan."

"And who is the captain? I must see him as soon as I am dressed."

"The cap is Wolf Larsen, or so men call him. But you better speak soft with him. He is mad this morning. The mate—"

Before he could finish, the cook had returned. "Better get out of here, Yonson" he said. "The old man will be wantin' you on deck. And this is no day to get him mad."

Johnson left quickly. The cook handed me a crumbled bundle of sour-smelling clothes. "These will have to do until yours dry out," he said.

As soon as I put the clothes on, my flesh was creeping and crawling from the rough contact. "I only hope you don't have to get used to these things in this life," he said. "I was pretty sure you was a gentleman as soon as I first saw you."

"And whom do I have to thank for this kindness?" I asked when I finished dressing.

"Mugridge, sir," he said. "Thomas Mugridge at your service."

"All right, Thomas," I said. "I shall not forget you—when my clothes are dry."

"Thank you sir," he said gratefully.

I stepped out on deck. Everyone seemed interested in what was going on amidships. A large man was lying on his back on the hatch. He was fully clothed though his shirt was ripped open in front. His eyes were closed and he seemed to be unconscious. His mouth was open, however, and he struggled to breathe. From time to time a sailor dumped a bucket of water over the man.

Pacing back and forth across the deck was the man whose glance had rescued me from the sea. He was five feet ten or so. But my first feel of the man was not of his height, but of his strength. He was a man of massive build, with broad shoulders and a deep chest.

The captain stopped pacing. He looked down at the dying man. As he did, the man put up a final struggle against death—and lost. The captain then let loose with a stream of foul language that shocked me. As far as I could tell, the man had been the ship's mate. He had gotten into trouble while the ship was in San Francisco and had become very ill. Now he had the bad taste to die and leave Wolf Larsen short-handed.

The captain stopped swearing as suddenly as he had begun. He started giving orders to bury the mate at sea. Finally he asked the hunters and sailors who had gathered on deck if anyone had a Bible or prayer book. No one spoke up.

"Then we'll drop him over without any service," he said. By this time he had turned completely around and was facing me.

"You're a preacher, aren't you?" he asked.

When I answered that I wasn't, he demanded, "What do you do for a living?"

I didn't know what to say. "I—I am a gentleman," I blurted out. He sneered at that. "I have worked, I do work," I went on.

"For your living?"

Before I could answer he said, "Who feeds you?"

"I have an income. But this has nothing to do with what I wish to see you about," I said.

He ignored my statement. "Who earned it? Eh? I thought so. Your father. You stand on dead men's legs. Let me see your hand." He stepped forward, gripped my hand and looked it over.

"Soft—good for little but dish washing."

"I wish to be put ashore," I said. "I'll pay you whatever you judge your trouble to be worth."

"I have a counter proposal for you," he said. "My mate is gone. There will be a lot of promotion. You take the cabin boy's place. Sign on for the cruise—$20 per month. You might learn to stand on your own two legs."

Before I could answer, Larsen turned to a young, strong-looking boy. "You, you're a boat-puller, now. You're promoted, see?"

"I didn't sign on for boat-puller, sir. I signed on for cabin boy. And I don't want to be a boat-puller."

When Larsen heard this, he sprung quickly across the deck and drove his fist into the boy's stomach. The boy collapsed in agony.

"Well?" Larsen asked me. "Are you going to take your duties as cabin boy?"

What was I to do? To be brutally beaten, maybe even killed, would do me no good. I looked steadily into Larsen's cruel, gray eyes.

"Yes, sir," I said.

"What is your name?"

"Humphrey Van Weyden," I answered.

"Age?"

"I am 35," I said.

"That will do. Go see the cook."

And so it was that I was forced against my will to work for Wolf Larsen.

For the rest of the day I learned my duties from the cook. His manner toward me changed greatly. Before, he had been polite because I was a "gentleman." Now, he was bossy and mean.

Later I served dinner at the cabin table to Wolf Larsen, the mate Johansen, and the six hunters.

My knee, which I had injured, was killing me. I got no sympathy from the men. But, as I was washing dishes, Wolf Larsen spoke up.

"Don't let a little thing like that bother you," he said. "It may cripple you some, but at the same time you'll be learning to walk."

That night as I lay in my bunk in pain, I thought about my situation. I, Humphrey Van Weyden, a man of art and letters, lying here on a Bering Sea seal-hunting schooner. Cabin boy! I had never done any hard manual work in my life. I had always been a bookworm. I had hated athletics and any violent activity. The doctors said that I had always had a strong body but had never developed it. I knew I was in no condition for the rough life ahead of me.

All the while, the schooner *Ghost* was rolling and plunging way farther into the heart of the Pacific. And I was on it. My mind ran wild, and I could not sleep. It was a long, long night—weary and dreary and long.

2 Life Aboard the *Ghost*

I had a very sleepless night. I awoke the next day weak and in great pain. Mugridge woke me at 5:30 A.M. and made a lot of noise doing it. The day was filled with a variety of awful experiences.

When I went to put my own clothes back on, I noticed my purse was empty. It had contained $185. I spoke to the cook about it when I went into the galley. I had expected a nasty answer— but I got much more.

"Look here," he began with a snarl in his throat. "Do you want your nose punched? If you think I'm a thief, just keep it to yourself, or you'll be sorry." And with that he put up his fists and started for me.

To my shame, I cowered and ran out the galley door. What else was I to do?

"Look at him run! Look at him run!" I could hear him cry. "Come on back, you poor little mama's darling. I won't hurt you."

I came back and went on with my work. After breakfast, I cleaned the stove and carried the ashes up on deck to empty them. Wolf Larsen and a sailor named Henderson were standing near the wheel talking. As I passed by them, I flung the ashes overboard. But stupidly I had thrown the ashes right into the wind. It drove them back, not only over me, but over Henderson and Larsen as well.

The next moment Larsen kicked me violently, as an animal is kicked. I had not realized that there could be such pain from a kick. I staggered away, leaned against the cabin and nearly fainted. I stayed there until the feeling passed.

Later that morning I received a surprise of a different kind. In cleaning up Larsen's stateroom I discovered a rack filled with books. I looked over the titles and was shocked. There were books by Shakespeare, Poe, and Tennyson, as well as scientific works by people like Charles Darwin. There were also books on astronomy and physics.

I could not figure this out. It was clear that this terrible man was no ignorant clod as one might have expected him to be. At once he became a puzzle. He clearly had two sides to him. And this glimpse I had of his other side made me feel bold. For later, I spoke up to him about the money I had lost.

"I have been robbed," I said.

"How did it happen?" he asked.

I told him about my clothes being left in

the galley and the cook's reaction when I mentioned it.

"The cook's pickings," he said smiling.

"How can I get it back?" I asked.

"That's your lookout," he answered. "You haven't any lawyer or business agent now. You'll have to depend on yourself. Besides, you left it around to tempt the cook, and he fell. You have placed his immortal soul in danger. Do you believe in the immortal soul?"

I halted. How could I explain my feelings to this man?

"What do you believe?" I asked, instead.

"I believe that life is a mess," he answered. "It's a thing that moves and may move for a minute, an hour, a year, or a hundred years. But in the end it will stop moving. The big eat the little so that they may move. The strong eat the weak so they may continue to be strong. The lucky eat the most and move the longest, that is all.

"It is piggishness," he went on. "Of what use is an immortality of piggishness? What is the end? What is it all about? Why move at all, since moving is living? Without moving there would be no hopelessness. But we want to keep on moving and living and dreaming of immortality. Bah! An eternity of piggishness!"

He turned suddenly and walked away. Then he stopped and asked, "By the way, how much did the cook get away with?"

"$185," I said.

He nodded and continued walking.

I began to learn more about the *Ghost* and its crew. The vessel was an 80-ton schooner, 23-feet wide and just over 90-feet long. It carried a crew of 22, along with seven boats. One was the captain's, and the rest were for the seal hunters to use. Each boat's crew was made up of a hunter, a boat puller, and a boat steerer.

Just about every man aboard seemed to have an excuse for having sailed on the *Ghost*. Most of the deepwater sailors claimed they did not know anything about the ship or its captain before they signed on. The hunters, who were excellent shots, were another story. They were well-known for being a troublesome bunch. It was said that no decent schooner would have taken them.

I made friends with one member of the crew. He was a rather heavy and friendly Irish chap named Louis. He loved to talk. One afternoon while I was peeling potatoes in the galley, Louis dropped in for a "yarn."

"Ah, my boy, this is the worst schooner you could've selected," he said, shaking his head.

"The mate was the first, but mark my words. There will be more dead men before the trip is done."

Then he went on to talk about the captain. "Listen to the word, will you. Wolf—that's what he is. He's not rotten some of the time. He is completely heartless. Wolf, just wolf, that's what he is."

My life working with Thomas Mugridge was becoming impossible. I had to address him as sir. On top of that, Wolf Larsen seemed to have taken a fancy to him.

My hands bothered me a great deal. They were not used to the hard work. I never before knew the meaning of those words. I had been resting all my life and did not know it. Now to have been able sit for one hour with nothing to do would have been heaven.

I did not dream that work was so terrible a thing. From 5:30 in the morning until 10:00 at night I was everybody's slave. For the first time in my life, I began to appreciate the working people.

After three days of light winds, we caught the northeast trades. I came on deck one morning to find the *Ghost* foaming along. Every sail was drawing except the jibs, and there was a fresh breeze astern. Oh, the wonder of the great trade winds. All day we sailed, and all night, and the next day, and the next. Day after day, the wind was always astern, blowing steadily and strong.

The days and nights were all a wonder and a wild delight. I had little time from all my work. But I sometimes would steal odd moments to look at the unending glory of what I never dreamed existed. The sky above was stainless blue—as blue as the sea itself. All around the horizon were pale, light clouds. They were like a silver setting for a perfect blue sky.

Sometimes I thought Wolf Larsen was mad, or at least half mad, what with his strange moods. At other times I took him for a great man, a genius. Finally, I was convinced he was a primitive man, born a thousand years too late. He was a man out of place, born into a century that had become too civilized for his like.

The 12:00 meal was over one day, and I had just finished putting the cabin in order. The captain and Thomas Mugridge came down the stairs.

"Get the cards, Hump," Larsen told me. "And bring out the cigars and whiskey from my berth."

They played cards for money. I do not know whether Larsen cheated or not, but he won steadily. The cook made repeated trips to his bunk for more money. And he continued to lose. Finally, when Mugridge had lost it all, he leaned his head on his hands and cried.

"Hump, kindly take Mr. Mugridge's arm and help him on deck," Larsen said to me politely. "He is not feeling very well."

"And tell Mr. Johnson to throw some buckets of water on him," he added in a low voice to me.

When I returned, Larsen had finished counting his winnings. "It comes to $185 even," he said. "Just as I thought. The beggar came aboard without a cent."

"What you have won is mine, sir," I said.

He looked at me strangely. "Hump, I have studied some grammar in my time. And I think your tenses are mixed up. You should have said, 'was mine,' not 'is mine.' "

"It is not a question of grammar, but of ethics."

"You are wrong," he answered. "It is neither a question of grammar nor ethics, but of fact."

"I understand," I said. "The fact is that you have the money."

His face brightened. He seemed pleased by my last statement.

"But it is avoiding the real question, which is one of right," I continued.

"Ah, I see you still believe in such things as right and wrong," he said.

"But don't you—at all?" I demanded.

"Not the least bit," he said. "Might is right, and that is all there is to it. Weakness is wrong. That is a poor way of saying that it's good to be

strong and evil to be weak. Or, it is better to be strong because of the profits, painful to be weak because of the losses. Just now my having this money is a good thing. I wrong myself if I give it to you. Then I give up the happiness of having it."

"But you wrong me by withholding it," I said.

"Not at all," he answered. "One man cannot wrong another man. He can only wrong himself. As I see it, I do wrong when I think of the interests of others. Don't you see?"

"I see you are a man one cannot trust to put aside his own selfish interests for a minute."

"Now you are beginning to understand," he said.

"You are a man totally without morals?"

"That's it."

"A man of whom to be always afraid—"

"That's the way to put it."

"As one is afraid of a snake, or a tiger, or a shark?"

"Now you know me," he said. "And you know me as I am generally known. Other men call me Wolf."

Time passed. Supper was at hand and the table was not set. I became restless and worried. Soon Mugridge glared down the stairs. I prepared to go about my duties. But Larsen cried out to him, "Cooky, you've got to hustle tonight. I'm busy with Hump, and you'll have to do without him."

That night I sat at the table with the captain and the hunters. Mugridge waited on us and washed the dishes. It was done because of Larsen's whim—a move which I knew would later bring me trouble. In the meantime the captain and I talked and talked. The hunters listened with disgust, for they could not understand a word of it.

3 A Nightmare of Brutality

I had three days of rest, three blessed days of rest. I ate at the captain's table and did nothing more than discuss life, literature, and the universe. All the while Thomas Mugridge raged and did my work as well as his own. But the three days of rest brought the trouble I expected.

It was plain that Mugridge was going to make me pay for those three days. He treated me horribly, cursed me, and heaped his work on me as well. He even once raised his fist to me. But I was becoming like an animal myself. When I snarled in his face, he backed off.

But then he found a new way to try to scare me. He took the one galley knife we had and sharpened it every chance he got. Soon, the whole crew was whispering, "Cooky's sharpening the knife for Hump." This talk pleased him endlessly.

One day the ex-cabin boy, George Leach, and Mugridge got into a violent argument. Before anyone knew it, Leach's right arm had been ripped open by a quick slash of the cook's knife. Leach took it calmly, but he gave the cook a warning. "I'm going to get you, Cooky. And you'll be without that knife when I come for you."

Several days went by. I could swear I saw the madness growing in Mugridge's eyes. And I became very much afraid. I knew I could not look to the captain for help in this matter. Whatever had to be done, I had to do for myself. So, I got the idea of fighting Mugridge on his own terms.

I got a knife from Louis and borrowed a sharpening tool from the mate, Johansen. The next morning Mugridge sat down in the galley and began to sharpen his knife. I stopped what I was doing and sat down opposite him. Then I pulled out my knife and began to do the same. To my surprise, he did not seem to notice what I was doing. He just kept on with his sharpening. So did I. For the next two hours we sat facing each other just sharpening away. Soon half the crew was looking down into the galley to see what would happen.

Nothing happened. At the end of the two hours Mugridge put away his knife and sharpening tool. Then he put out his hand.

"What's the good of makin' a show for these mugs," he said. "They'd be very glad to see us cutting up our throats. You're not half bad, Hump. You got spunk. So, come on and shake."

I might have been a coward, but I was less a coward than he. I had won a clear victory. And I refused to make it less by shaking his hand.

"All right, take it or leave it," he said. Then he shouted up at the crew to get away from the galley.

"I see Cooky's finished," I heard Smoke say to Horner.

"You bet," came the answer. "Hump runs the galley from now on."

As the days went by, those remarks proved to be true. I did my own work only and in whatever way I saw fit to do it. I carried my knife with me all the time. My attitude toward Mugridge had changed. I no longer feared him. In fact, I paid him no attention at all.

It had become clear to me how lonely a man Wolf Larsen was. There wasn't a man aboard who didn't fear or hate him. Nor was there a man aboard whom Larsen himself didn't hate. The loneliness was bad enough. But he also seemed to have a constant sadness about him. When he laughed, it was never from happiness. It was just another expression of the rage and strength that was inside him.

He had begun to suffer from bad headaches. One morning I went into his cabin to straighten up. His head was buried in his hands and he was groaning, "God! God! God!" I softly left the room. At dinner he asked the hunters for something to relieve headaches. By that evening, he was half blind and reeling about the cabin.

"I've never been sick in my life, Hump," he said as I helped him to his room.

The blinding headache lasted three days. He suffered as wild animals suffer. He didn't complain, got no sympathy, and suffered alone.

When I entered his room on the fourth day, I found him well and hard at work. He was using a compass and square to copy a scale of some sort.

"Hello, Hump," he greeted me in a friendly way. "I'm just finishing it up. Want to see it work?"

"What is it?" I asked.

"A labor-saving device for seafarers. It will allow a child to navigate a ship." Then he showed me how it worked.

"You must be excellent in mathematics," I said when he finished. "Where did you go to school?"

"Never saw the inside of one," he answered. "I had to dig it out for myself."

As I continued to make up the room, I found myself looking at him. He was certainly a handsome man. He had a clean-shaven face, with clear lines and sharp features. The sea and sun had tanned his fair skin to a dark bronze.

The set of his mouth, his chin, his jaw, was firm. So was the nose. It was the nose of a person born to conquer or command.

The mystery of this man forced me to speak up. "Why is it that you have not done great things in this world?" I asked. "With the power that is yours, you might have risen to any height. Instead, here you are, living a dirty life hunting sea animals. What was wrong? Did you lack ambition? Did you fall under temptation?"

He waited a moment before answering. Then he went on to tell me about his early life. He was born on the west coast of Norway. His parents were poor, uneducated Danish people. They came from a long line of poor, uneducated people. They made a small living off the sea. And from his youngest days, Larsen and all his brothers were forced into the same kind of life.

One by one Larsen's brothers went off to sea and never came back. At the age of 12, Larsen joined the English merchant service. He advanced quickly, from cabin boy at 12 to able seaman at 17. It was while sailing in the merchant fleet that Larsen taught himself to read and write. He had been educating himself in navigation, mathematics, science, and literature ever since.

I told him that history was filled with those who started out as he had and had risen to do great things.

"And history tells of opportunities that came to those who rose to great things," he said. "No man makes opportunity. Napoleon knew that. I have dreamed as greatly as Napoleon. I should have had the opportunity, but it never came. Well Hump, you now know more about me than any living man except my own brother."

"And where is he?" I asked.

"Master of the steamship *Macedonia*, seal hunter," he answered. "We will meet him probably on the coast of Japan. Men call him Death Larsen."

"Death Larsen!" I cried. "Is he like you?"

"Hardly. He is a lump of an animal without any head. He has all my—"

"Brutishness?" I said.

"Yes, all my brutishness, but he can hardly read or write. And he is happier for leaving life alone. He is too busy living it to think about it. My mistake was in ever opening the books."

The next day a horror of brutality swept across the ship. Wolf Larsen was really the cause of it. There were such hard feelings among the men because of him that things were bound to explode.

Thomas Mugridge started it. He told the captain that seaman Johnson had been complaining that he'd been cheated at the ship's slop chest. The slop chest was a kind of small dry-goods store which all sealing vessels carried. It was stocked with whatever things the sailors might need during a voyage. They bought the goods and the money was taken out of their future earnings.

It seemed Johnson had bought some oilskins from the slop chest that he felt were of poor quality. And he made no secret of his feelings. When word got back to the captain, he called Johnson and the mate Johansen to his cabin. I was present when they came in.

"Shut the doors and draw the slide," Larsen said to me.

I did as I was told and saw the fearful look on Johnson's face. Still, I did not dream of what was to come. Johnson knew and awaited it bravely.

"Johnson, I understand you're not quite satisfied with those oilskins?" Larsen began.

"No, I am not. They are no good, sir."

"And you've been shooting off your mouth about them."

"I say what I think, sir."

"Do you know what happens to men who say what you've said about me and my slop chest?"

"I know, sir," Johnson said.

"What?" Larsen demanded sharply.

"What you and the mate are going to do to me, sir."

"Look at him, Hump," Larsen said. "What do you think of him?"

"I think that he is a better man than you are," I answered. Somehow I wished to take some of the anger directed at Johnson and put it on me.

"Do you know what I am going to do?" he asked.

I shook my head.

"Watch me."

He left his chair from a sitting position, springing from it like a wild animal. He landed on Johnson with all the fury of an attacking tiger.

I cannot fully describe the horror that followed. It makes me sick even now to think of it. Johnson fought bravely. But he was no match for Wolf Larsen, let alone Larsen *and* the mate.

Finally, after they had beaten him senseless, Larsen told the mate to ease off.

"Jerk open the doors, Hump," Larsen said.

I did. Then the two brutes picked up the senseless man like a sack of rubbish. They heaved him up the stairs and onto the deck. George Leach dragged Johnson forward. Then he went about dressing his wounds and making him comfortable. Johnson's face was so swollen and discolored that he did not look like himself.

Later Larsen came up on deck. He stood smoking a cigar and checking the log. I was standing on deck myself trying to recover from what I had seen. Suddenly Leach's voice came to me. When I saw him, he was standing below on the port side of the galley. His face was white with rage. His eyes were flashing, and his clenched fists were raised overhead.

"May God send your soul to hell, Wolf Larsen," he cried. "Only hell's too good for you, you coward, you murderer, you pig!"

I was shocked. I waited for Larsen to attack Leach. But he didn't. He just walked over to the top of the galley and looked down at the boy.

Leach continued raging at the captain. "Pig! Pig! Why don't you come down and kill me?" he shouted. "You can do it! I'm not afraid."

Just then Mugridge walked out the galley door and passed Leach. He turned to the youth and said, "Such language! Shocking!"

Now Leach's rage had a new target. And for the first time since he'd stabbed him, the cook was without his knife. Leach knocked him down hard. Three times he got up, and three times he was knocked down again.

Finally, the cook began to yell. "Oh, Lord! Help, help! Take him away! Take him away!"

The hunters began to laugh from pure relief. The sailors crowded around grinning and shuffling to watch the hated cook get his. And even I felt a great joy within me. Only the expression on Wolf Larsen's face never changed.

He just stared at the happenings with a curious look.

The beating Leach gave the cook was almost as bad as the one Johnson had gotten. No one broke it up. Finally, Leach stopped the pounding and walked off. Mugridge was left on the floor, whimpering and wailing like a puppy.

These two beatings were only the opening events of the day's program. Later, two of the hunters fired shots at one another in the steerage area. They wounded each other and angered Wolf Larsen so much that he beat them both before he dressed their wounds. Still later, the mate Johansen and the hunter Latimer got into a fight. The cause of it seemed to be the noises made by the mate during his sleep.

The whole day had been like some horrible dream. One cruel act had followed another. My nerves and mind were shocked. I had never in my life witnessed man's brutality to man. That night I tossed and turned on my bunk between one nightmare and another.

4 A Murderous Plot

For three days I did my own work and Thomas Mugridge's as well. And I'm not bragging when I say I did his work well. I know that it won Wolf Larsen's approval. The sailors also smiled with satisfaction during the time I was in charge.

Three days was all Larsen allowed Mugridge to recover from his beating. On the fourth day he was pulled from his bunk by the back of his neck and sent to his duty. He was lame and sore, and he could hardly see. He sniffled and wept, but Wolf Larsen was without sympathy.

Several more days passed before Johnson crawled on deck. Then he went about his work in a half-hearted way. He was still a sick man, and more than once I observed his pain. Worse, it seemed that his spirit was broken. He followed orders from Larsen and Johansen as if he were a slave. Leach, however, was a different story. He went about like a tiger cub. He showed his hatred of the captain and Johansen openly.

Wolf Larsen had another bad attack of headaches, which lasted two days. He must have suffered badly. When he called me in, he obeyed my commands like a sick child. But nothing I could do seemed to help. Why such a great animal as he should have headaches at all puzzled me.

"It's the hand of God, I'm telling you," Louis warned. "It's to pay back for all his evil deeds. And there's more coming."

"But still no more dead men," I teased.

He shook his head sadly. "Trouble's a comin', I tell you. It's close, it's close. And it will be stand by all hands when it begins."

The brutishness of these men made me think that I had never placed a proper value upon women. My mother and sisters were always about me, and I was always trying to escape them. They were forever worried about something. If they weren't after me about my health, they were trying to straighten out the "mess" of my room. Suddenly I missed them very much. I was sure if I ever got home I would never be angry with them again.

All this had me thinking about the men of the *Ghost*. Where were the mothers of the 20-odd men on this ship? It was not natural or healthy for men to be totally separated from women for so long a time. It brought about the cruelty and brutality I had just seen.

These men should have had wives, sisters, daughters. Then they would have been capable of softness, tenderness, and sympathy. But not one of them was married. For years and years not one of them had been in contact with a good woman. There was no balance in their lives.

One night I decided it was too stuffy to sleep below. It was a calm night. We were out of the trades, and the *Ghost* was moving ahead at just over a knot an hour. So I tucked a pillow and blanket under my arm and went up on deck.

Harrison was at the wheel. As I passed by him, I noticed he was a full three points off course. I thought perhaps he had fallen asleep. But his eyes were wide open and staring. He seemed greatly worried.

"What's the matter?" I asked. "Are you sick?"

He shook his head and then caught his breath.

"You better get on your course then," I said.

I took my bedclothes and began to move on again. Then some movement caught my eye. I looked over and saw that a wet hand was clutching the rail from below. As I watched, a second hand took hold. At first, I couldn't make out the form that was climbing aboard. Then, the eyes and face of Wolf Larsen appeared before me. His right cheek was red with blood. It was flowing from some wound in the head.

He drew himself together and stepped toward me. I shrank back, for I saw the look of death in his eyes.

"All right, Hump," he said. "Where's the mate?"

When I shook my head, he called out. "Johansen, Johansen." No answer.

"Where is he?" he demanded of Harrison.

"I don't know, sir," he answered. "I saw him go forward a little while ago."

"So did I go forward. But as you can see, I didn't come back the way I went. Can you explain it?"

"You must have been overboard, sir."

"Come on, Hump," the captain said. "We won't find the mate. But you'll do."

I followed at his heels. We found three sailors asleep on watch. When Larsen questioned them, they claimed they had just fallen asleep. They said they hadn't seen anything happen on deck.

Larsen told me to be quiet. Then we went down into the forecastle. I had not been down there before. It was shaped like a triangle and was quite small. Yet there were 12 bunks there in a double tier. It smelled sour and old. And every bit of wall space was covered with something—sea boots, oilskins, clothes, what have you.

Larsen went over to the sleeping men one by one. He began checking their pulses to see if they were really asleep and how long they had been that way. In doing this, he might learn who had been on deck when he went overboard.

The first few men he checked were clearly sleeping and had been for some time. Then

Larsen walked over to where Leach's and Johnson's bunks were, top and bottom.

Larsen reached down to take Johnson's pulse. I was standing behind him holding the sea lamp. I could see Leach's head rise slowly to see what was going on. All at once, the lamp was dashed from my hand and the room went dark. At the same instant, Leach leaped straight down on Larsen.

A moment later, the room was in an uproar. Johnson and some of the others joined in the fight. I leaned against the ladder, too frightened to do anything. I could not see a thing. But I could hear the force of the blows and the shouts of the men. It was clear that several of them were involved in this plot to murder Larsen and Johansen, the mate.

"Get a knife, somebody!" Leach was yelling.

"Pound him on the head," Johnson cried. "Mash his brains out."

The struggle continued. Leach was pleading for someone to give him a knife. After a while there were so many men fighting in the dark, they hurt their own cause. Larsen was able to fight his way across the floor to the ladder.

No man other than a giant could have done what he did. He gained the foot of the ladder. Then step by step he climbed up, all the time with the pack of men trying to drag him down.

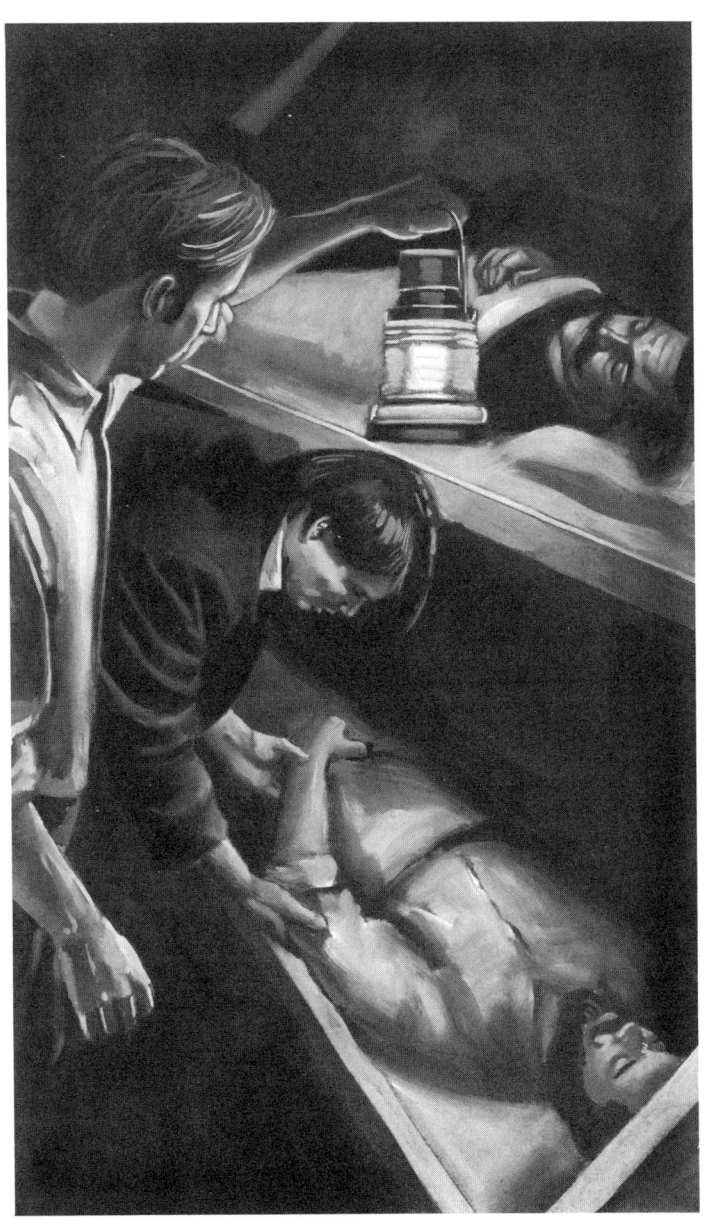

From up above, Latimer had gotten a lantern and was shining it down. "Who is it?" he cried.

From half way up the ladder, I could hear the low voice of the captain. "Larsen," he said.

Latimer reached down with his free hand and Larsen grabbed it. He kicked his feet at the men still clinging to his body. One by one they began to fall away. Finally, Larsen and the lantern disappeared upstairs.

There was a good deal of cursing and groaning as the men crawled to their feet. Soon, everyone was blaming each other for their failure. Leach kept saying, "And not one of you got a knife."

The men were worried that Larsen would surely take revenge on them. Everyone knew there was trouble ahead. But it was clear from the talk that they expected Johnson and Leach to catch the most of it. In fact, the others considered those two already dead.

A moment later Latimer called down that the captain wanted me in his cabin. When I came out of hiding, some of the men tried to stop me. They thought I would tell Larsen what I'd overheard. But Leach, bless him, stuck up for me.

"Let him go," he ordered.

"Not on your life," one sailor said.

"Let him go," Leach repeated. "I tell you, he's all right. He doesn't like the old man any more than you or me."

I found Larsen in his cabin. He was stripped and bloody, waiting for me. "Come, get to work, doctor," he said. "It looks like you'll get a lot of practice on this trip."

I must say I bandaged his wounds well. I was surprised that they weren't that bad. When I finished, Larsen said, "Hump, you are a handy man. As you know, Johansen is gone, and we're now short a mate. From here on, you'll stand watch and receive $75 a month. And you shall be called Mr. Van Weyden."

"I don't understand navigation, you know."

"Not necessary at all."

"I don't care for the position," I went on.

He smiled as if it were all settled.

"I won't be mate on this hell ship!" I cried out.

His face grew hard. He walked to the door and said, "Now, good night Mr. Van Weyden."

"Good night, Mr. Larsen," I said weakly.

5 Rescued from a Storm

The position of mate did carry with it one great advantage for me. There were no more dishes to wash! But I was ignorant of the easiest duties of the mate. I was lucky the sailors sympathized with me. They all took pains to help me with the ropes and the rigging of the sails.

As the days went by, I found myself taking a secret pride in myself. It was a hard-to-believe situation—a landlubber as second in command of the ship. But I was carrying it off well. And I grew to love the heave and roll of the *Ghost* under my feet as it moved north and west.

For the rest of the crew, however, things were horrible. Wolf Larsen would never forget the attempt on his life and the beating he had received. Morning, noon, and night he tried to make life unlivable for the crew.

As was expected, life was worst for Johnson and Leach. Both men would have killed Larsen if they had the slightest chance. But they never got one. Larsen and Leach engaged in one terrible fight after another. Leach was always the loser. Sometimes he'd even wind up knocked out cold on the deck. But that never stopped him from fighting again with the hated captain.

I often wondered why Larsen did not kill him and put an end to it. But he seemed to enjoy it. "It gives a thrill to life," he explained to me.

"But it is cowardly," I cried. "You have all the advantage."

"Of the two of us, you are the greater coward," he answered. "If you were true to yourself, you would join forces with Leach and Johnson. But you are afraid. You want to live at all costs."

There was a bitter truth in what he said. I lost much sleep over it. I even talked with Johnson and Leach about it. Both men had lost hope, but Leach clasped my hand in friendship.

"I think you're square, Mr. Van Weyden," he said. "But stay where you are and keep your mouth shut. We're dead men; I know it. But you might be able to do us a favor sometime."

The next day we put in at Wainwright Island to fill our water barrels. I had hoped that both men might have a chance to escape then. But Larsen had chosen his spot well. We lay half a mile beyond the beach, which was surrounded by deep mountain walls no man could climb.

Late that afternoon we pulled anchor and sailed away. Nothing was before us but three or four months of hunting on the sealing grounds.

The mood on the *Ghost* was almost like that of a funeral.

Finally, we reached the coast of Japan and caught up with the great seal herd. We traveled north with it, destroying the poor animals. We flung their carcasses to the sharks and salted down the skins, all so that they could later be placed upon the fair shoulders of city women.

It was my job to count the skins as they came aboard. I was also supposed to oversee the skinning and later the cleaning of the decks. My soul and my stomach were disgusted by the work. And yet, this job toughened me up in a way that was good for someone with my "soft" background.

I saw more of Wolf Larsen now than ever before. When the hands were away on the boats, only he, Mugridge, and I were left on board. It was our job to sail the *Ghost* to a point the boats could get to quickly if the weather turned bad.

We had several days of good weather. Then one morning the boats went out early. Larsen looked to the eastern sky and became worried.

"Old Mother Nature is going to get up on her hind legs and howl," he said. "It will keep us jumping, Hump, just to pull through with half our boats. You better go up and loosen the topsails."

Soon the wind began strengthening and the sea began to rise. I steered for an hour, each moment becoming more difficult.

"Now use the glasses and spot some of the boats," Larsen told me.

The weather grew worse. "Expect all hell to break loose," Larsen warned me. "But don't mind it. Do your own work and have Cooky stand by the foresheet."

The *Ghost* suddenly changed course. We went right into the full force of the wind. A huge wave rose above us. Then it came crashing down upon the ship. My body struck and pounded the deck as the ship was tossed about. Somehow, Larsen was still at the wheel pitting his will against the will of the storm.

The captain was finally able to straighten the ship out. By some miracle, it was still in working order. I spotted one of our boats about 20 feet away. After a great deal of work, we were able to bring the boat and its three men aboard.

Soon I sighted a second boat. It had turned over, and was resting bottom up. Clinging to it were Jock Horner, Louis, and Johnson. We pulled the boat aboard along with its grateful crew.

We spent the rest of the afternoon looking for our boats. When we saw the number four boat, the crew was nowhere to be seen. But Larsen was set on recovering the boat at all costs. The

seas were very rough. When we finished the job, one of the men, Kelly, was still missing.

That night all hands assembled in the cabin. Hot coffee and food were never so welcome. The ship was still being tossed about violently.

"To hell with a lookout," Larsen said when we'd eaten. "There's nothing that can be done on deck. All hands turn in and get some sleep."

Before we left, I said to him, "It wasn't worth it. A broken boat for Kelly's life."

"But Kelly didn't amount to much," he answered coldly. "Good night."

The next day, the storm blew itself out. We began sighting and boarding other sealing ships in the area. We were looking for our remaining lost boats and crews, as were they. After five days we were short only four men—including Kelly.

We set out again to hunt the seals. At this time, Leach came up to me and spoke in a low voice. "Can you tell me, Mr. Van Weyden, how far we are off the coast? And what are the bearings of Yokohama?"

I gave him the information. "Thank you, sir," was all he said.

The next morning the number three boat, Johnson, and Leach were missing. Wolf Larsen was furious. He set sail after the runaways. Larsen paced the deck like an angry lion.

On the morning of the third day, a cry came that the boat had been sighted. I felt sick knowing what Larsen planned to do to the men. I must have lost my senses. I grabbed a loaded shotgun from steerage and headed back up on deck.

Suddenly another cry rang out, "There's five men in that boat!"

I was so thankful. I quickly put the gun away and went up on deck.

The boat had gotten closer. It was larger than any sealing boat and built differently. One of the hunters began to laugh. "Talk about a mess," he said.

"What's wrong?" I asked.

Again he laughed and pointed at the boat. "Look there in the stern sheets, on the bottom. May I never shoot a seal again if that's not a woman!"

He was right. I could now see that the boat contained four men and a woman. Everyone became excited. All except Wolf Larsen. He was clearly disappointed that the boat was not his boat with Leach and Johnson on board.

I took no part in helping the newcomers aboard. I was busy with my other duties. Then Wolf Larsen's voice brought me to attention.

"Mr. Van Weyden! Will you take the lady below and see to her comfort? Make up that spare port cabin. Put Cooky to work on it."

I was almost afraid of the woman. It had been so long since I had been in the company of one. I was nearly shocked by her smallness and softness.

I seated her in Wolf Larsen's chair. "No need to go to any great trouble for me," she said. "The men were looking to spot land at any moment this morning. The vessel should be in by night, don't you think?"

I was shocked by her faith in quickly finding land. I answered her honestly.

"If it were any other captain except ours, you would be in Yokohama by tomorrow," I said. "But our captain is a strange man. Be prepared for anything, understand? For anything."

"I must say I do not understand," she said. "We are so close to land, you know."

"Honestly, I do not know," I said. "I want to prepare you for the worst, if the worst comes. This captain is a devil. One can never tell what his next act will be."

She asked no more questions. I went about making her as comfortable as I could. After a while, she fell asleep right in the chair. I covered her with a blanket and put a pillow under her head. Then I left.

6 Death in the Water

When I came up on deck, I learned we had sighted Leach and Johnson's boat. The seas had turned rough again. Wolf Larsen soon appeared, looking bright and happy. He had been talking with the men we'd rescued.

"Three oilers and an engineer," he said. "But we'll make sailors out of them, or boat pullers anyway. Now, what of the lady?"

I just shrugged my shoulders.

"What's her name?" he demanded.

"I don't know," I answered. "She is asleep. She was very tired. What vessel was it?"

"The *City of Tokyo*, a mail steamer," he said. "Bound for Yokohama from San Francisco. Disabled in the typhoon. The five of them were at sea for five days. And you don't know who or what she is—maid, wife, or widow? Well, well."

"What do you plan to do to Leach and Johnson?" I said, changing the subject.

He shook his head. "Really, Hump, I don't know. With these new men, I've got about all the crew I want."

"And they've had about all the escaping they want. Why not give them a change in treatment?

Take them back and deal with them gently. Whatever they have done, they have been hounded into doing."

"By me?"

"By you," I answered boldly. "And I warn you, Wolf Larsen. I may forget my own life in my wish to kill you if you keep on mistreating them."

"Bravo!" he cried. "You do me proud, Hump! You've found your legs quite nicely. I like you better for it. Do you believe in promises?" he asked.

"Of course," I said.

"Suppose I promise not to lay my hands upon Leach and Johnson. Will you in turn promise not to try and kill me? Not that I'm afraid of you," he added.

I could hardly believe my ears. What was coming over this man?

"Is it a go?" he asked.

"Yes," I answered.

The boat was close at hand now and in a bad way. Johnson was steering and Leach was bailing water. Larsen signaled for the *Ghost* to get close. Leach and Johnson looked up into the faces of their shipmates who had lined the rails. There was no greeting. The two men were dead in their shipmates' eyes.

Suddenly, the boat was gone astern. It got caught in the wind of our sail and nearly capsized. Leach kept bailing water and Johnson was clinging to the oar.

For the next hour the small boat tried to get alongside again. Finally, it did. "So, you've changed your mind?" I heard Larsen cry out. "You want to come aboard, eh? Well then, just keep coming."

Then he gave order upon order that moved our vessel farther away. All the time he kept waving his arm for the two helpless men to follow along.

Johnson came after us. There was nothing else he could do. It was only a matter of time before one of the huge waves would roll over the boat and drown the men.

Then a thick sheet of rain hid the boat from view. It never came back out. The wind blew the air clear, but the boat's sail could not be seen. I thought for a second I saw in the distance the boat's black bottom. But as for Johnson and Leach, the sea had swallowed them up.

As I walked along the deck, I was approached by one of the men we had rescued. His face was white, his lips trembling.

"Good God, what kind of a ship is this?" he cried.

"You have eyes, you have seen," I answered with a heavy heart.

I went up to Larsen. "Your promise?" I said.

"You'll agree I did not lay a hand on them," he said. "Far from it, far from it," he laughed.

We learned the woman's name from the engineer—Miss Brewster. She slept until the following morning and then joined us at breakfast. Wolf Larsen had little to say to her at first. But she spoke right up to him.

"And when shall we arrive in Yokohama?" she asked directly.

"In four months, possibly three if the season ends early," he answered.

She caught her breath. "I thought Yokohama was only a day away," she said. "It's not right."

"You can speak to Mr. Van Weyden about what is right," he said. "He is an expert on such things."

I dropped my eyes and my face flushed under her stare. It was cowardly, but what else could I do?

"I may be taken off by some passing vessel perhaps," she said.

"There will be no passing vessels except other sealing schooners," he said.

"I have no clothes, nothing," she said. "You hardly realize, sir, that I am not a man. And I'm not used to your careless way of life."

"The sooner you get used to it the better," he said. "I'll give you cloth, needles, and thread. I hope it will not be too much of a hardship for you to make a dress or two."

She made a strange face. It was clear she was frightened and confused.

"I suppose you are like Mr. Van Weyden there," Larsen went on. "You are used to having things done for you. What do you do for a living? Do you feed yourself? Or does someone else feed you? Have you ever earned a dollar by your own labor?"

"Yes I have," she answered. "At present I earn about $1,800 a year."

All eyes rose up to her. Larsen was clearly impressed.

"Well, Miss Brewster, that's about $150 a month. Consider yourself on salary during the time you remain with us." He paused. "I forgot to ask. What tools do you need to do your work?"

"Paper, ink, and a typewriter," she answered.

"You are Maud Brewster," I said slowly as if I were charging her with a crime.

"How do you know?"

"I remember writing a review of a thin little book—"

"You!" she cried. "You are—"

I nodded.

"Humphrey Van Weyden," she finished. She sighed with relief. "I am so glad."

We were soon off on our own conversation. She was a well-known author. As a critic I had reviewed her works. A strange fate indeed had thrown us together so far from our shores.

The hunters left the table. Only Wolf Larsen stayed. Suddenly I became aware that he was still there. "Oh, don't mind me," he laughed. "I don't count. Go on, go on."

But the gates of speech were closed. We got up and left the table as well.

Wolf Larsen's anger at being left out of our conversation had to come out somehow. And it fell to poor Mugridge to bear the cost.

Larsen was angry that the cook had not changed his dirty ways. So he ordered that he be given a "tow over the side." Mugridge was caught, tied up, and dropped over the side.

Fifty or sixty feet of line were run out. The rope tightened, the *Ghost* plunged onward, and the cook was jerked to the surface. On and on it went. Although he couldn't drown, each lift and dunk made him feel as if he were half drowning. Yet the crew was laughing heartily.

Maud Brewster came up beside me. She hadn't seen Mugridge in the water yet. She wanted to know why everyone was laughing. I told her to ask Captain Larsen.

Suddenly a cry came out. "Shark ho, sir."

"Heave in, lively," Larsen shouted.

Mugridge was screaming wildly. I could see a black fin cutting the water and heading for him. Just before Larsen could pull him completely aboard, the shark came up. Mugridge cried out and then hit the deck with a splash.

A fountain of blood was gushing forth. His right foot was missing, cut off neatly at the ankle. Maud Brewster had turned white and was staring right at Larsen.

"Man-play, Miss Brewster," he said. "A little rougher that I expected. The shark was not in the plan."

She turned away, a look of hatred in her eyes.

Mugridge buried his teeth in Wolf Larsen's leg. The captain calmly pressed his fingers at the rear of the man's jaws and his mouth flew open.

"Will you dress the wound, Mr. Van Weyden," he said and walked off.

7 A Silent Understanding

Later that day Maud Brewster came up to me when I was alone. I made sure no one could hear us.

"What is it?" I asked.

"I can understand that this morning was mostly an accident," she began. "But I have been talking with Mr. Haskins from my vessel. He tells me that the day we were rescued two men were drowned—on purpose. Murdered."

"Yes, that is correct," I said. "They were murdered."

"And you let it happen!" she cried.

"I was not able to prevent it from happening."

"Did you try?"

When I didn't answer, she said, "But why not?"

"You must remember, Miss Brewster, you are new to this world. You do not yet understand the laws which operate here."

She shook her head in disbelief.

"What would you suggest then? Should I take a knife, or a gun, or an ax and murder this man?"

"No, not that!" she cried.

"Then what should I do? Kill myself?"

She did not answer.

"What remains? Mine is the role of the weak. I remain silent and suffer in disgrace, as you will remain silent and suffer, too. It is the best we can do if we wish to live. We don't have the strength to fight this man. If we win, we must do it with our brains.

"We must stand together, but do so secretly," I went on. "I shall not be able to side with you openly, no matter what happens. And you must take no action on my behalf either."

"Still I do not understand," she said. "What shall I do then?"

"Don't make an enemy of this man. Be friendly with him. Talk with him, discuss literature and art—he is fond of such things. He is a good listener and no fool. And try to avoid seeing as much of the brutalities on board as you can."

Suddenly, I saw Larsen coming toward us. I quickly turned the conversation. "The editors were afraid of him and the publishers would have none of him," I said.

"We were talking of Harris," I said to Larsen as he came up to us.

"Oh, yes," he said. "I remember his work. You better look in on Cooky, Mr. Van Weyden. He's complaining and restless."

Later, when I returned to the deck, I saw that Miss Brewster had followed my advice. She was having a friendly talk with Larsen.

We continued to drive into the heart of the seal herd. And Miss Brewster continued to have long talks with Wolf Larsen on deck. I have to say that I had become completely charmed by her. And that is not strong enough a word to describe my feelings.

One morning she and Larsen came toward me as I stood above the galley entrance. Though she tried to hide it, I could see fear in her eyes. She looked at me and then quickly looked away.

It was in Larsen's eyes that I saw the cause of her fear. Usually, his eyes were gray and cold and harsh. Now they were soft and golden and seemed to have lights dancing in them. It was clear that the glow had been put there by Miss Brewster.

Her own fear rushed in on me. And in that moment, I knew that I was in love with her. I looked back into the eyes of Larsen. He had recovered. The color and lights were gone. They were once again cold. He turned away and walked by me.

"I am afraid," she whispered with a shiver. "I am so afraid."

I too was afraid. But I answered calmly. "All will come right, Miss Brewster. Trust me, it will come right."

Two days later a cry came down from above. "Smoke, ho!"

"How's it bear?" Larsen cried out from below.

"Dead astern, sir."

"Maybe it's a Russian," Latimer said.

His words brought fear to the hunters. If the approaching ship was Russian, that meant we had gone too close to forbidden waters.

"We're safe," Larsen said with a laugh. "But I'll lay a bet that it's the *Macedonia*."

"Then I'd like to make a run for it anyway," Latimer answered. "There's never been a time when there wasn't trouble when you and that brother of yours got together."

Everyone smiled, including Larsen.

When we all went up on deck, we could see the steamer getting closer. We lowered our boats, and they spread out. The seals were thick and the wind was dying away. Everything favored a big catch.

"Where is the trouble you were expecting, Captain?" Miss Brewster said.

"What did you think? That they'd come aboard and cut our throats?" he answered.

"Something like that," she said. "I don't know what to think. And what could be worse than cutting our throats?"

"Cutting our purse," he said.

"I fail to see that this steamer has any plans to cut your purse," she said.

"Wait and you will see," he said.

We didn't have long to wait. The *Macedonia* passed several miles beyond our line of boats. Then it lowered its own. We knew it had 14 boats to our 5. It began dropping them in such a way as to take away our chance at any seals. There were no seals behind us. And like a huge broom, the *Macedonia's* boats now swept up all the seals ahead of us.

There was nothing to be done. Our boats headed for home. A lot of angry men came back aboard our ship. Each man felt he had been robbed. The boats were brought aboard amid many curses. And if those words had any power, Death Larsen would have been buried under them for all time.

8 Escape!

"You've been on deck, Mr. Van Weyden," Larsen said to me the next morning at breakfast. "How do things look?"

"Clear enough," I answered.

"What of the *Macedonia*?" he asked.

"Not sighted," I said.

He looked disappointed. Soon the call came from the deck above, "Smoke, ho." Larsen's face grew brighter. "Good," he said.

He left the table, and soon Maud and I could hear Larsen's voice coming from the steerage. We couldn't tell what he was saying. But whatever it was brought forth great cheers from the hunters.

We went up on deck. The hunters had come out carrying their shotguns and their rifles. The sailors were lowering the boats. They set a northerly course for us to follow.

"What's up?" I asked Wolf Larsen.

"I'm going to give that brother of mine a taste of his own medicine," he said.

Larsen steered the wheel with one hand. With the other, he used the glasses to study the position of our boats and the *Macedonia*. Our boats were rowing as well as sailing. Even the hunters were pulling. In short time, they quickly overtook the *Macedonia*'s five hunting boats. The smoke of the mother ship itself had nearly disappeared from the horizon.

Soon the *Ghost* bore down upon the first of the five boats. When we got closer, the three men in it looked up at us. Larsen greeted them with a friendly wave. "Come on board and have a gam," he cried. Among sailing schooners, a "gam" is a friendly visit between crews of different ships.

The three men came aboard. The hunter was huge, at least six feet eight or nine inches. He clearly felt he had nothing to fear from Wolf Larsen. Larsen invited him below. The other two men went forward to do their own visiting.

A moment later the sounds of a great struggle came up from below. It was like a battle between a leopard and a lion. The lion made all the noise. It was obvious that Wolf Larsen—the leopard—was winning.

The sounds soon died away. Then Larsen came back on deck. He showed no signs of the battle. He called over to the other two men.

"Hoist in your boat," he said to them. "Your hunter has decided to stay aboard awhile. He doesn't want the boat pounding alongside."

The two men didn't move. "Hoist in your boat, I said," Larsen said sharply. "Who knows? You may have to sail with me for a time."

This time the men obeyed. After it was done, Larsen returned to the wheel. Then he set our course after the *Macedonia's* second hunting boat.

We spent the next few hours pursuing and capturing the *Macedonia's* boats. What the *Ghost* did not go after, our hunting boats attacked. By late afternoon we had picked up all five of the boats. However, we were not home free yet. The *Macedonia* had reappeared and its captain knew what we had done. He set out after us.

Death Larsen's ship, belching the blackest of smoke, came charging down upon us. Its mission was to catch the *Ghost* and retake its five boats.

A puff of smoke broke forth from the *Macedonia's* deck. We heard a heavy sound, and a round hole took form in the stretched canvas of our mainsail. They were shooting at us with a small cannon!

They kept on firing. When the two ships were a half mile apart, a shot made another hole in our mainsail. Then suddenly we entered the fog. It was all about us, hiding us in its dense, wet gauze.

Wolf Larsen squared the ship away and ran along the edge of the fog bank. His trick was clear to see. He had entered the fog and was forcing his brother to come in and out after us. But finding us would be like finding the old needle in a haystack. And he knew time was on our side.

"He can't keep this up," Larsen said. "He'll have to go back for the rest of his boats."

He was soon proved right. We had escaped with the *Macedonia's* crew and five boats. Larsen had paid his brother back for his stunt the day before.

Larsen was thrilled. "We must make these newcomers welcome, Mr. Van Weyden," he said. "And I'll bet you each one is hunting as happily for me tomorrow as they did for my brother yesterday."

That night the entire crew celebrated. There was much drinking, yelling, and laughing. Larsen, as could be expected, was in a great mood. But he himself did no drinking. He and Maud engaged in another long talk, this one on the subject of desire. After she left, he turned to me.

"I'll relieve Louis at the wheel," he said. "Then I'll call upon you to relieve me at midnight. Better turn in now and get some sleep."

I do not know exactly what woke me up later that night. But I found myself out of my bunk and wide awake. And my soul was shaking to the warning of danger.

I threw open the door to my cabin. I saw Maud, my Maud, trying to push herself away from Wolf Larsen. She was struggling in his arms and he was almost crushing her. I sprang forward.

I hit him with my fist on his face, but it was a small blow. He roared like an animal and shoved me away. I was hurled backward against the door.

I struggled to my feet and grabbed my knife. But something had happened. Larsen and Maud were apart. She was leaning against the wall for support. Larsen was staggering, his left hand pressed against his forehead and covering his eyes. I sprang upon him, blindly, crazily. I drove the knife into his shoulder. I knew the blow was no more than a flesh wound. I raised the knife to strike a more serious blow. But Maud cried out, "Please don't. For my sake."

"I would kill him for your sake," I cried.

"Please don't," she said.

I looked at Larsen. His body had gone limp. His head was bowed. His hand still covered his eyes.

"Van Weyden, Van Weyden, where are you?" he cried.

"Here I am," I answered. "What is the matter?"

"I am a sick man, Hump," he said. "Help me to

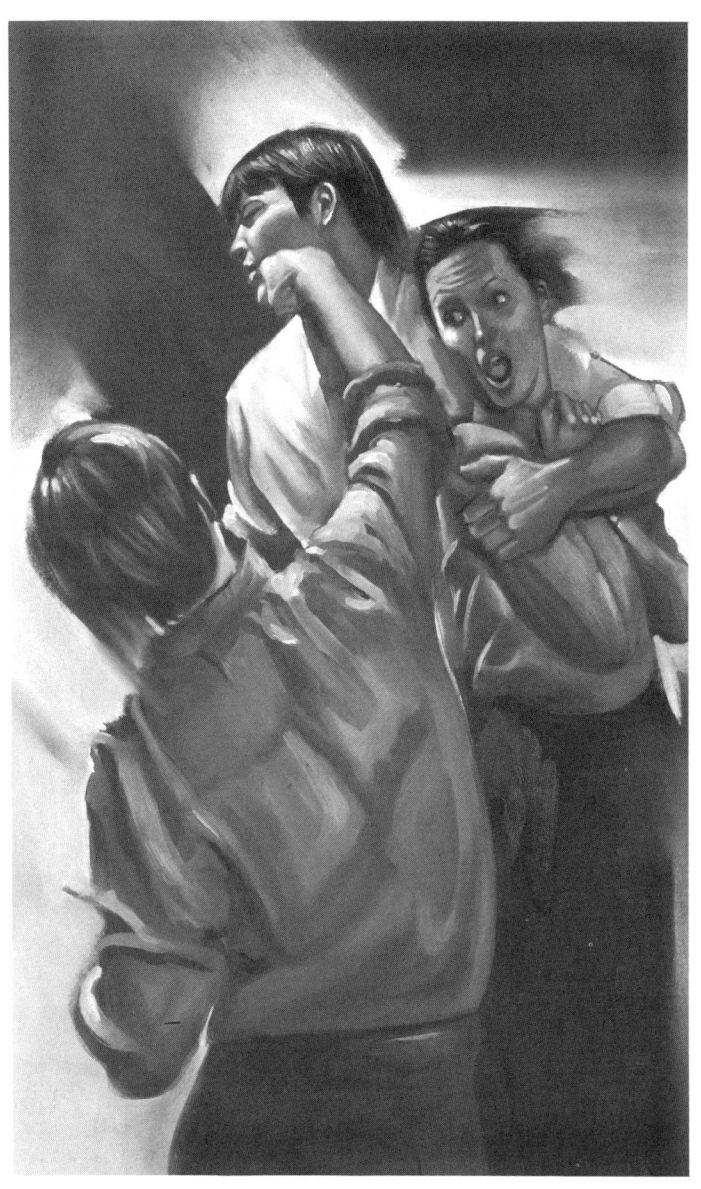

my bunk. It's those headaches. Help me to my bunk."

I did as he asked. Then I returned to Maud. "Will you trust yourself to me for a journey of 600 miles?" I asked.

"You mean—?" she asked.

"Yes, I mean just that," I answered. "There is nothing left for us but the open boat. Dress as warmly as you can. Make a small bundle of what you wish to take with you. And please hurry."

I took as many provisions as I could find. Then with some difficulty I lowered a boat. No one on deck came close enough to see us. I helped Maud over the rail, then followed her into the boat.

"There lies Japan, straight before us," I said.

We turned our heads to see the last of the *Ghost*. Soon, all sight and sound of it faded away. We were alone on the dark sea.

Day broke, cold and gray. There was a fresh breeze blowing. My fingers were cold and they hurt from gripping the oar all night. And my feet were stinging from the pain of the frost.

Maud lay before me in the bottom of the boat. She was warm, for she had thick blankets over and under her. She began to move about, and finally her eyes opened.

"Good morning, Mr. Van Weyden," she said. "Have you sighted land yet?"

"No," I answered.

"How far do we have to go?"

"Siberia lies off there," I said pointing to the west. "But to the southwest, some 600 miles away, is Japan. If this wind holds, we should make it in about five days."

We had a cold breakfast. Then Maud insisted that I teach her how to steer. I tried to tell her that I hardly knew how to myself. This was my first time in a small boat. Still, she wanted to learn so she could relieve me at times.

After I had given her a lesson, she spread out the blankets and ordered me to sleep. I must have been exhausted, for I didn't wake again until 1:00. I'd slept for seven hours!

Now Maud was very tired and sore from steering for so long a time. I scolded her for not waking me sooner. She promised she wouldn't do it again.

The rest of the day passed without problems. We took turns steering and standing watch in our boat. I was unafraid. I no longer feared death. I forgot my own life in the love of another. And yet, I never wanted to live so much as right then.

9 Endeavor Island

There is no need to tell at length of our suffering in the small boat during our many days at sea. We faced one storm after another. The wind beat in our faces and the white seas roared by. Neither of us slept much. All the time we were being driven off to the northeast, directly away from Japan and toward the bleak Bering Sea.

Throughout it all, I found myself more in love with Maud than ever. The declaration of my love trembled on my tongue a thousand times. But I knew it was no time for such a statement.

During one of the worst storms, I glanced off to the leeward side. I hadn't expected to see anything. I could hardly believe my eyes. In the distance, I saw land! It's black point stuck up from the raging surf that pounded its base.

"Maud," I said pointing to it.

"It cannot be Alaska!" she cried.

"No," I answered. "Can you swim?"

She shook her head.

"Neither can I," I said. "So we must get ashore without swimming. We must find an opening

between the rocks through which we can drive the boat."

I thought we would surely crash into the rocks. But we didn't. As we got closer, we began to hear a huge bellowing sound rising above the surf. We passed the point, and a cove came into view. There, the white sandy beach was covered with seals. It was from them that the bellowing came.

"A rookery!" I cried. "Now we are saved. There must be men and cruisers to protect them from the seal hunters. Perhaps there is a station ashore."

We managed to get through the rough seas and slide into another cove. I jumped out and gave my hand to Maud. She reached for it, and then nearly collapsed onto the sand. At the same time I swayed and nearly fell myself. After so long on the sea, the stable land was a shock to us.

"I really must sit down," Maud laughed.

I made the boat secure and joined her. We had landed on Endeavor Island.

We spent the first day resting and waiting for the storm to pass. I pitched a tent for Maud, and found a way to a build a fire using gunpowder. We were finally able to have some hot food—and coffee!

I wanted to take the boat and explore the island myself. But Maud insisted on going with me. I was convinced we would find some men stationed there to protect all the seals. Maud thought we had discovered some unknown rookery.

"If you are right, we must prepare to spend the winter here," I said. "Our food will not last. But there are the seals. They go away in the fall. So, I must soon begin to lay in a supply of meat. We have to build huts and gather driftwood. We will have our hands full if we find the island without people. Which we shall not, I know."

But she was right. We sailed all along the shore searching the coves with our glasses. Once in awhile we landed, but could find no signs of human life anywhere.

We completed our trip by early afternoon. I figured the island's circumference was about 25 miles, and its width between 2 and 5 miles. The island was highest at its far southwestern point. The northeastern part rose only a few feet above the sea. There were at least 200,000 seals in the area.

We returned to our little cove greatly disappointed. After dinner, I returned to the boat to sleep. But I lay awake that night, staring up at the stars. On the *Ghost*, I had learned to be responsible for myself. Now for the first time in my life, I found myself responsible for someone else—the woman I dearly loved.

For two weeks we worked at building a hut. Maud helped a great deal. It pained me to see her bruised, bleeding hands. But I was proud of her.

We used stones for the walls, and that part went smoothly. The roof was the problem. I could use the spare oars for the beams, but what could we cover them with? Grass or moss would never do.

"I've read that someone used the skins of a walrus," I said.

"There are the seals," Maud suggested.

So the next day the hunting began. I did not know how to shoot, but I learned. However, it took me 30 shells to kill the first three seals. It became clear that I would use up all the ammunition before I could kill what we needed.

"We must club the seals," I announced. "I have heard the sealers talk about clubbing them."

"They are so pretty," Maud objected. "I cannot think of it being done. It is so much more brutal than just shooting them."

"The roof must go on," I said. "Winter is almost here. It's our lives against theirs."

Maud and I went out together. The "lord" of the harem of seals was quite protective of them. I aimed a blow at one of them, and I heard Maud shout, "Look out." When I turned around the lord was charging down upon me. I had to flee.

Finally, I was successful at learning which seals to approach without putting myself in danger. Shouting and making threatening movements with my club, I attacked the "lazy" ones. By the end of the day, I had killed and skinned enough to cover the hut's roof.

10 An Unwelcome Visitor

The second hut was easier to build. I built it against the first so only three walls were necessary. But it was hard work, all of it. Maud and I labored from dawn to dark, to the limit of our strength.

We held a housewarming in my hut the night the roof was finished. It was the end of the third day of a huge storm. The wind whistled and bellowed about the hut. At times I feared it would collapse. Yet we remained warm and comfortable. We had gotten used to the idea of being on the island for the entire bitter winter.

"Something is going to happen," Maud said finally. "Something is coming to us."

"Good or bad?" I asked.

She shook her head. "I don't know, but it is there somewhere." She pointed toward the sea.

"I'm sure I'd rather be here than arriving on a night like this," I said laughing. "You are not frightened?"

Her eyes looked bravely into mine.

We talked a little longer before she went.

"Good night, Maud," I said.

"Good night, Humphrey," she said.

The use of our first names had come about naturally. I was left alone in my hut glowing warmly through and through. Something had begun to exist between us that had not existed before.

I awoke the next morning with an odd feeling. I got dressed and opened the door. I heard the waves hitting the beach. The sun was shining. I stepped outside with a new energy.

When I was outside, I stopped short. I couldn't believe my eyes. There on the beach, not 50 feet away, was the *Ghost*. The masts lay alongside. Nothing seemed to be moving on board.

I knew Maud and I could never escape. My first thought was to board the ship, creep into Wolf Larsen's bunk, and kill him right there. My knife was at my hip. I returned to my hut and got my loaded shotgun. Then I went down to the *Ghost*.

The hunting boats were missing. The forecastle and steerage were empty. The ship was deserted. It was Maud's and mine, I thought.

I sprang up the break of the poop deck—and saw Wolf Larsen. He stood staring straight at me, but he made no movement whatever.

Neither of us spoke. I pointed my gun at him and began to tremble. Had he moved I most surely would have shot him. But he just stood there and stared at me.

"Well," he finally said. "Why don't you shoot?"

I cleared my throat.

"You can't do it," he said. "In spite of what I've taught you, you can't kill an unarmed man."

"I know it," I said weakly.

"And you know I would kill an unarmed man as easily as I would smoke a cigar. Bah, I had hoped better things of you, Hump," he said.

He came up to me. "Put down that gun. I want to ask you some questions."

He then went on to ask me what island we were on, where Maud was, and how the *Ghost* was lying. He said the seals had awakened him. He knew he had stumbled upon a rookery—and he was thrilled.

"Thanks to my brother, I've come upon a fortune," he said.

I asked him what happened to the crew.

"My brother got me within 48 hours," he said. "He boarded me in the night with only the watch on deck. He gave the hunters a better offer, and everyone deserted me."

"How are your headaches?" I asked.

"They still trouble me," he said. "I think I have one coming on now."

He slipped down onto the deck and rolled over on his side. He spoke no more. I left him and went down into his stateroom. I took all of his guns. Then I checked the steerage and forecastle for any other weapons. I went into the galley and picked up all the knives there. I also grabbed some dishes and a frying pan. Then I went back up on deck. Larsen was just as I had left him.

I returned to my hut and fixed breakfast. Presently Maud came in. She hadn't looked at the beach. But she did notice the dish from which she was eating. She looked at me, and then she slowly turned toward the beach.

"Humphrey!" Terror mounted in her eyes. "Is he here?" she cried.

I nodded my head.

We waited all day for Larsen to come ashore. But he did not even come on deck. The next day we waited, and the next, and still he made no sign. It was a horrible period of waiting for us.

"It's these headaches of his," Maud said on the fourth day. "Maybe he is ill. Or even dying."

"Better so," I said.

"But think, Humphrey, a fellow creature in his last lonely hour. We must do something."

"Perhaps," I said.

"You must go aboard and find out," she said.

I picked up my gun. "Do be careful," she said.

When I reached the ship's deck, I took off my shoes. I found the cabin deserted and the door to Larsen's stateroom locked. I lifted the trapdoor leading below and set it aside. I went down to get some things from the storeroom. When I came back up, I saw Larsen come out of his stateroom.

He was groaning. "God, God!" he cried out. His hand swept across his eyes. He fought to pull himself together. After a great struggle, he did.

Now I worried about the open trapdoor. When he saw it, he would know I'd come aboard. I rose up, gun in hand. But he took no notice of me. And he didn't notice the open trap. In fact, he walked right into the opening. As he fell, he grabbed the side and was able to pull himself clear.

He dropped the trapdoor into place, closing the opening. Suddenly I understood. He thought he had me trapped below. I also noticed that he was blind—as blind as a bat.

I watched him quietly. He stepped quickly to his stateroom. His hand missed the doorknob the first time he reached for it. I had my chance. I tiptoed across the cabin to the top of the stairs. I watched Larsen return with a heavy sea chest. He placed it on top of the trapdoor. Then he got a second one and did the same.

When he finished, he went into the galley to cook for himself. I gathered up the things I had taken from the storeroom. Slipping quietly past him, I climbed down to the beach. Then I went to make my report to Maud.

11 Repairing the *Ghost*

"It's too bad the *Ghost* has lost its masts," Maud said. "We could sail away in it. Don't you think we could, Humphrey?"

I jumped up, excited.

"It can be done, it can be done," I said. "We can put the masts back into the *Ghost* and sail away."

"But how can it be done?" she asked.

"I don't know," I said. "I only know I feel I can do anything these days."

"But there is Captain Larsen," she said.

"Blind and helpless," I said.

"But those terrible hands of his. You told me how he leaped across the trapdoor opening."

"I also told you how I crept about and escaped him," I reminded her.

We began to make plans for repairing the ship's masts. We walked down to look at the *Ghost* more closely. When I saw the huge masts lying in the water, the job did seem much too great. Still, we were determined.

The next morning Maud and I went into the hold of the *Ghost* to begin our work. We had just started, when the sound of our work brought Wolf Larsen out.

"Hello below!" he cried down the open hatch.

"Hello on deck," I answered. "Good morning."

"What are you doing down there?" he demanded to know. "Trying to wreck the rest of my ship?"

"Just the opposite," I answered. "I'm trying to repair it. I'm getting everything ready to replace the masts."

"It seems you're standing on your own legs at last, Hump," he said. "But I say you can't do it."

"Oh yes I can," I said. "I'm doing it now."

"But this is my ship, my property. What if I forbid you?"

"Wolf Larsen," I said. "I am not able to shoot a helpless, unarmed man. We both know that. But I warn you. I will shoot you the moment you try one hostile act. I can shoot you now as I stand here."

"Just the same, I forbid you from working on my ship."

"But don't you care to escape this island?" I asked in disbelief.

"No," he answered. "I plan on dying here."

"Well we don't," I said. I went on with my work.

The next day we ran into some problems. It took us all day to work them out. By late afternoon when I straightened up, I was in quite a bit of pain. However, I looked proudly at my work.

"I wish it weren't so late," I said. "I'd like to see how this works."

"Tomorrow will be soon enough," Maud said. "You're so tired now you can hardly stand."

"And you?" I said. "You must be very tired. You have worked just as hard."

Maud smiled. "If our friends could see us now."

We returned to our huts and had supper. "We worked hard all day," I said. "It's a shame we can't have a full night's sleep."

"But there can be no danger now? From a blind man?" Maud asked.

"I shall never be able to trust him," I said. "I trust him even less now that he is blind."

The next morning after breakfast, we went aboard the *Ghost*. Our hearts sank. During the night, Larsen had slashed and cut through most of what I had spent the past few days putting together. And worse, he had cast adrift the lines that had held the masts, booms, and gaffs.

"He deserves to die," I cried out. "And God forgive me that I'm not man enough to do it."

"Things will work out," Maud said. "We are in the right, and things will work out."

Suddenly we saw Larsen strolling along the poop deck. "Take no notice of him," I whispered.

"He's coming to see how we take it. Don't let him know that we know. We can deny him *that* satisfaction."

Then we played hide-and-seek with the blind man. But he knew we were on board. "Good morning," he said at one point. "I know you're aboard." Then he listened closely for us to reply or make movements. We did neither.

We continued this game for awhile. Then Larsen left the deck in disgust and returned to the cabin. We climbed down from the deck back into the boat. I looked into Maud's clear brown eyes and forgot the evil Larsen had done. I only knew that I loved her. And because of her the strength was mine to win our way back to the world.

It took us three days to find the missing masts. We searched far and wide in our little boat for them. With a great effort, we made several trips towing the masts, booms, and gaffs back to the *Ghost*.

On the fourth day I slept until three in the afternoon. I woke up to find Maud cooking dinner. Her powers of recovery were amazing.

It took me another three days to undo much of the damage Larsen had caused. That night I slept on board, beside my work. Maud slept in the forecastle. During the day Larsen had sat about listening to my work. But he made no comments, and he made no further demands that I stop.

In the middle of the night I heard footsteps on deck. I rolled out of my blankets and silently followed Larsen about. He was armed with a knife that I must have forgotten to take from the ship. He walked over to the riggings and drew his weapon.

"I wouldn't if I were you," I said quietly.

He heard the click of my pistol and laughed.

"Hello, Hump," he said. "I knew you were here all the time. You can't fool my ears."

"That's a lie," I said. "However, I am aching for a chance to kill you. So go ahead and cut."

"I'd rather disappoint you," he answered. He laughed and walked away.

The next morning Maud and I discussed the problem. We decided something had to be done about him. If he was free to move about, he could do anything. He might set the vessel on fire or try to sink it. We had to make him a prisoner. But how?

Just then Larsen came out on deck. He was walking strangely. He stumbled and staggered as he reached for something to hold on to. Then he collapsed and sank to the deck.

"One of his attacks," I whispered to Maud.

She nodded. I could see the sympathy for him in her eyes.

We went up to him. He seemed to be out cold. But when I took his pulse it seemed quite normal. Suddenly, his hand moved and grabbed my wrist like a steel trap. I cried out loud. His face had a look of triumph on it. He pulled me toward him and held my arms so I could not move.

His free hand went around my throat. I felt the taste of death. I couldn't see, but I heard Maud turn and run quickly across the deck. A long moment later, Larsen sank under me. His grip on me was released, and I could breathe again. I rolled over onto the deck and looked up. Maud was looking down at me with both fear and relief. In her hands was a heavy seal club. The brave woman had saved me!

She began to tend to Larsen's wound. "No," I said. "Now we have him helpless. And he shall remain that way. From this day on we live in the cabin. Wolf Larsen lives in the steerage."

We dragged him below and placed him on a lower bunk. Then I remembered that he had handcuffs in his stateroom. I got them, and we handcuffed his feet and hands. For the first time in days, I breathed freely.

12 A Return to the Open Sea

The next afternoon Larsen showed signs of recovery. Maud brought him some food. When she tried to talk to him, he moved about. But he made no reply to her. That's when we discovered he was deaf in his right ear.

"Do you know you are deaf in the right ear?" I asked him when he was fully awake.

"Yes," he answered in a strong, low voice. "It's worse than that. My whole right side is affected. It seems asleep. I cannot move arm or leg."

"Are you faking again?" I demanded angrily.

"That was the last play of the Wolf," he said. "I am paralyzed. I shall never walk again.

"It's too bad," he went on. "I'd have liked to have done you in first. I thought I had that much left in me."

"But why?"

"Oh, just to outlive you. To be the biggest bit to the end, to eat you. But to die this way—"

"How do you explain your condition?"

"The brain," he said at once. "Those cursed headaches brought it on. I was never sick in my life. But something has gone wrong with my brain. A cancer, a tumor. Something that destroys the nerve centers, cell by cell.

"The curse of it is that I must lie here and watch it all happen," he went on. "I am mentally fine. But I cannot see. Hearing and feeling are leaving me. Soon, I will not be able to speak. I shall be here, alive, active, and powerless."

"Yes, but your soul.... Don't forget the power of the soul."

"Bosh!" he said. "I can remember and I can think and reason. When that goes, I am no longer here. The soul?" He broke out in laughter. Then he turned his good ear to the pillow in a wish to stop the conversation. We left him alone.

The days went on. Maud and I continued making the *Ghost* fit for sailing. We removed Larsen's handcuffs. He suffered another stroke. He lost his voice, and it only returned at certain times. A harsh winter hit the island. I worked on, slowly making progress.

The day the mast was lifted and put into place was wonderful. Maud and I stood on the deck, so very proud of all that we'd done. Suddenly, I could smell something burning. Smoke was pouring from the steerage area.

"The Wolf is not dead yet," I said to myself as I raced below.

He had set the mattress of the bunk above on fire. The room was very smoky. I grabbed the burning mattress. Then I ran back up for some fresh air. It took several buckets of water to put the fire out.

Larsen was out cold. But the fresh air soon brought him around. He asked for some paper and pencil. "I am smiling inside," he wrote. "You see, I am still a bit of the old Wolf."

"I'm glad you're as small a bit as you are," I said.

"Thank you," he wrote.

We continued to care for Wolf Larsen as best we could. Then the day came for our departure from the island. The *Ghost's* stumpy masts were in place, its crazy sails bent. My work wasn't pretty, but it was strong. I knew it would hold.

We slipped the anchor, and Maud hoisted the sail. I cleared both the inner and outer coves, and the *Ghost* headed out to open sea.

I steered all day and through the night. I ate very little. Soon I was beginning to fall asleep at the wheel. Finally, Maud guided me to the cabin. I slept for 21 hours. When I awoke it was seven in the morning. I went up on deck. The *Ghost* was doing quite well on its own with its sails out.

I found Maud in steerage by Larsen's bunk. I looked down at him. There were no signs of life.

"He had too great a strength," I said.

"Yes," she said. "But now it no longer chains him. He is a free spirit."

The next morning we buried Wolf Larsen at sea. "I remember only one part of the service," I

said. 'And the body shall be cast unto the sea.' "

"Good-bye, proud spirit," Maud whispered.

As we walked back along the deck, I happened to look toward the east. A few miles away I could see a small steamship. It was heading toward us. I recognized it as a United States ship.

"We are saved," I said. "I hardly know whether to be glad or not." We looked at each other. And before I knew it, my arms were around her.

"Need I tell you?" I asked.

"There is no need," she said. "But the telling of it would be so very sweet."

I kissed her. Then I looked toward the vessel. It was very close. A boat was being lowered.

"One more kiss before they come," I whispered.

Maud just smiled—the most wonderful smile I had ever seen. It was a smile full of love.